D1209281

Good Manners in a Restaurant

by Katie Marsico
illustrated by John Haslam
Content consultant: Robin Gaines Lanzi, PhD, MPH,
Department of Human Science, Georgetown University

visit us at www.abdopublishing.com

Published by Magic Wagon, a division of the ABDO Group, 8000 West 78th
Street, Edina, Minnesota, 55439. Copyright © 2009 by Abdo Consulting Group,
Inc. International copyrights reserved in all countries. All rights reserved. No part
of this book may be reproduced in any form without written permission
from the publisher.

Looking Glass Library™ is a trademark and logo of Magic Wagon.

Printed in the United States.

Text by Katie Marsico
Illustrations by John Haslam
Edited by Amy Van Zee
Interior layout and design by Becky Daum
Cover design by Becky Daum

Library of Congress Cataloging-in-Publication Data
Marsico, Katie, 1980-
  Good manners in a restaurant / by Katie Marsico ; illustrated by John Haslam.
    p. cm. — (Good manners matter!)
  Includes bibliographical references (p.   ) and index.
  ISBN 978-1-60270-609-5 (alk. paper)
  1. Table etiquette—Juvenile literature. 2. Restaurants—Juvenile literature. I.
Haslam, John. II. Title.
  BJ2041.M368 2009
  395.5'3—dc22

                          2008036319

Contents

Why Do Good Manners Matter in a Restaurant?

You and your soccer team have just sat down in the best pizza restaurant in town. You're starving! The server is about to take your order. Should you tell her to hurry up and bring your pizza right away?

In a restaurant, servers take your order. You should be polite and patient with them. Say "please" when you ask for food and "thank you" when they bring it to you. Don't yell at them or rush them.

If you've been in this situation, you know it's important to use good manners in a restaurant. That means being polite to the server. Can you guess why good manners matter in a restaurant?

You should also be polite to the people at your table. This means not eating the entire pizza yourself! Make sure everyone else has enough before you take seconds.

Imagine a trip to the pizza restaurant without good manners. People might be shouting their orders at once. You might not even get a slice of pizza! The people at your table would only be thinking about themselves. They would grab as much food as they could.

You wouldn't like going to restaurants very much if people were this rude. Let's think about how you can practice good manners in a restaurant.

Show Good Manners in a Restaurant!

Eating in a restaurant is a chance to relax and talk to your friends and family. Don't talk with your mouth full of food. Be sure to wait for someone else to finish speaking before you do. You will do a much better job sharing your thoughts and ideas if you talk clearly and listen well.

Eating isn't the only thing to do in a restaurant. By politely talking and listening, you can show others that you care about them. That makes you fun to be around!

Remember to wait until the server brings everyone's plate to the table before you begin eating. This shows respect for the people you are eating with. How would you feel if you didn't have your food and the people around you were munching away?

What are other good manners you can use at restaurants? Always sit up straight in your booth or chair. Keep your elbows off the table. Put your napkin on your lap and use it to wipe your mouth or hands.

Sometimes you can't help burping after a tasty meal. Just cover your mouth and then say "excuse me" after. You can often stop yourself from burping by eating slowly. You will enjoy your food more if you do this, too!

What about the clothes you wear? It might be alright to wear everyday clothes to your favorite pizza place. But, you should dress in nice clothes when you visit fancy restaurants. You can always ask your parents if you're unsure how to dress.

You can also ask an adult if you are unsure how to eat. You can use your hands to eat some foods, such as pizza and hamburgers. Other foods, such as pasta and soup, must be eaten with silverware.

What should you do if you want the bowl of salad that's at the other end of the table? Ask the person sitting closest to the bowl to pass it to you. Remember to say "please" and "thank you."

Having good manners in a restaurant means respecting everyone around you. This includes diners who are eating at other tables. Don't shout or run in a restaurant. This might bother people who are trying to enjoy their meals.

There are lots of ways to practice good manners in restaurants. Let's see those good manners in motion!

Manners in Motion

Kayla and her brother, Sam, were going with Aunt Kim to a new restaurant in the city. They were both excited. But what should they wear? Kayla decided to ask her mom.

"You will be at a very fancy restaurant," Mom said. "You should wear a nice skirt or dress. Sam should wear his dress pants and a shirt that buttons in front." Kayla and Sam each had on their best clothes when Aunt Kim picked them up.

They carefully watched Aunt Kim once they arrived at the restaurant. They listened to how she spoke to the server.

"Can you please bring us some water and three chicken specials?" she asked the server. "Thank you!" Aunt Kim next unfolded her napkin and placed it in her lap. Kayla and Sam did the same thing. Everyone at the table took turns talking about their favorite foods while their meals were prepared.

Then the server brought out their plates. Kayla and Sam wiped their mouths and hands with their napkins during dinner. They also never spoke if they were chewing food. They each ate slowly and enjoyed their meal. Aunt Kim had a surprise for them when they finished.

"How about we share a piece of cake?" she asked. "I think you both deserve a treat for having such good manners!"

Can you name all the different ways Kayla, Sam, and Aunt Kim practiced good manners in the restaurant? Having good manners is easy! Just remember to be polite and show respect for everyone who is eating and working around you. What good manners have you practiced in a restaurant lately?

Amazing Facts about Manners in a Restaurant

Excuse Me!

You probably try to practice good manners by not burping after your meal. You would not have to excuse yourself if you burped in China though! People in China think it's good manners to burp after a meal. They feel burping is a way to show you are grateful for your food and that you enjoyed it.

How about Washing Those Hands?

Why do parents always ask you to wash your hands before dinner? It is bad manners to come to the table with dirty hands. You may think that your soccer friends won't care if you have dirty hands when you share a pizza. But, washing your hands helps get rid of germs that spread illness. Show you have good manners and keep everyone healthy by using some soap and water!

Top Five Tips for Good Manners in a Restaurant

1. Don't talk with your mouth full of food.
2. Place your napkin on your lap.
3. Use the silverware at the table for foods you do not eat with your hands.
4. Don't run, shout, or complain about the food.
5. Don't forget to say "please," "thank you," and "excuse me!"

Glossary

polite—showing good manners by the way you act or speak.
respect—a sign that you care about people or things and want to treat them well.
rude—showing bad manners by the way you act or speak.
server—a waiter or waitress who takes your order in a restaurant.
silverware—items such as forks, spoons, and knives that you use to eat food.

Web Sites

To learn more about manners, visit ABDO Group online at **www.abdopublishing.com**. Web sites about manners are featured on our Book Links page. These links are routinely monitored and updated to provide the most current information available.

Index